WRITTEN, DRAWN AND CREATED BY
MIKE BARFIELD

EDITED BY JONNY LEIGHTON

DESIGNED BY ZOE BRADLEY

COVER DESIGN BY JOHN BIGWOOD

WITH A LITTLE HELP FROM THESE GREAT FIGURES ...

FRIDA KAHLO

PABLO PICASSO

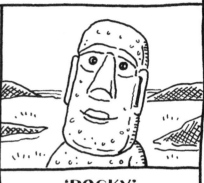

'ROCKY'

AND NOT FORGETTING THESE ONES, EITHER ...

MIKE BARFIELD

'BUTTERCUP'

YOU IN YOUR STUDIO

FOR ALICE

First published in Great Britain in 2019 by LOM ART, an imprint of
Michael O'Mara Books Limited, 9 Lion Yard, Tremadoc Road, London SW4 7NQ

W www.mombooks.com/lom   f Michael O'Mara Books   🐦 @OMarabooks   📷 @lomartbooks

Copyright © Mike Barfield 2019

Layout copyright © Michael O'Mara Books Limited 2019

A CIP catalogue record for this book is available from the British Library.

ISBN: 978-1-912785-07-0

1 3 5 7 9 10 8 6 4 2

This book was printed in January 2019 by Leo Paper Products Ltd,
Heshan Astros Printing Limited, Xuantan Temple Industrial Zone,
Gulao Town, Heshan City, Guangdong Province, China.

CONTENTS

ABOUT THE AUTHOR

Mike Barfield is a writer, cartoonist, poet and performer. He has worked in TV and radio, as well as in schools, libraries, museums and bookshops. He is the creator of the *Destroy This Book* series.

INTRODUCTION

Packed into these pages is a whole gallery of arty projects to POP OUT, and even more to cut out, stick, fold, colour in and doodle on, all inspired by famous art and artists.

Complete your own mini-masterpieces and have a whole load of fun in the process. There are fab facts to feast upon and tasty nuggets of know-how to digest, too.

You don't need any expensive or hard-to-find craft supplies to start your art. Pens, pencils, scissors and glue cover most of the projects, plus a few paper clips and paper fasteners. (The beret and silk scarf are optional.)

GLUE

SCISSORS

PENS & PENCILS

STICKY TAPE

PAPER CLIPS
& FASTENERS

ARTY CLOTHES
(OPTIONAL)

☆ NOW IT'S TIME TO GET CREATIVE!

OFF THE WALL

MAKE THIS ANCIENT ART COME ALIVE

AUROCH

RHINOCEROS

MAMMOTH

Cave art dates back roughly 14,000 to 40,000 years ago. Painted in dark caves by firelight, it often depicts animals. Some, like aurochs and mammoths, are now extinct.

Coloured using powdered minerals, experts think flickering flames would make the pictures appear to move. Try making your own cave wall horses move below.

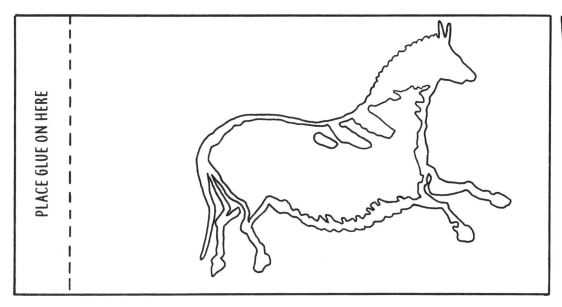

STICK FOLDED FLAP ON TO HERE

These horses are depicted in the Lascaux Grotto in France. Colour them in using earthy browns and reds, and then turn the page.

PLACE GLUE ON HERE

NEXT!

1. After colouring in both horses, cut them out.

2. Lay the short piece on top of the longer one.

3. Fold over the flap and glue.

4. Roll the top sheet around a pencil.

5. Roll the pencil back and forth.

6. The horse appears to move.

GET THE PICTURE?

This is a simple form of flipbook. Your eye combines the two images to give you the illusion of one horse moving.

ARTY ARMY

The 'Terracotta Army' is the name given to over 7,000 life-size clay statues of soldiers found buried in a tomb in China in 1974.

 They were sculpted on the orders of China's first emperor, Qin Shi Huang (259–210 BCE).

 Amazingly, no two figures have the same face – though one appears twice below. Can you spot which one?

秦始皇

THIS FIGURE IS OVER 1.8 M TALL!

THIS FIGURE IS A GENERAL. ALL THE STATUES ARE NOW GREY, BUT THEY USED TO BE VERY BRIGHTLY PAINTED. COLOUR HIM IN.

DRAW MORE FACES IN THE GAPS.

WHICH WAY UP?

This bowl of vegetables comes from an oil painting by Italian artist Giuseppe Arcimboldo (1527–1593), who was famous for his paintings of fruit and veg.

Turn it upside down to reveal the big-nosed and bearded 'vegetable gardener'.

COLOUR IN THE PICTURE.

Switchable pictures like this are fun to create. Many involve pairs of faces. Frown lines become mouths; hair becomes a beard; hats become collars, and vice versa!

CAN YOU DRAW YOUR OWN TOPSY-TURVY HEAD?

☆ Is this a young princess or an old lady?

SCARY!

HAIRY!

☆ Is this man feeling happy or angry?

☆ NOW GIVE IT A GO YOURSELF.

8

SPIN THE RAINBOW

Artists mix paints to create thousands of different colours and shades.

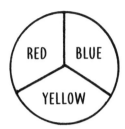

The three 'primary' colours — red, blue and yellow — can be mixed in pairs to give three 'secondary' colours — purple, orange and green.

CLAUDE MONET (1840–1926) USED A WOODEN PALETTE TO MIX OIL PAINTS BEFORE APPLYING THEM TO A CANVAS.

Mixing primary and secondary colours produces six 'tertiary' colours, all of which have places on the colour wheel below. Each secondary and tertiary colour is a blend of its two neighbours.

☆ **COLOUR IN THE WHEEL FOLLOWING THE KEY, THEN POP IT OUT AND TURN THE PAGE.**

KEY:

PRIMARY
1. Red
2. Yellow
3. Blue

SECONDARY
4. Orange
5. Green
6. Purple

TERTIARY
7. Vermilion (red-orange)
8. Amber (yellow-orange)
9. Chartreuse (yellow-green)
10. Teal (blue-green)
11. Violet (blue-purple)
12. Magenta (red-purple)

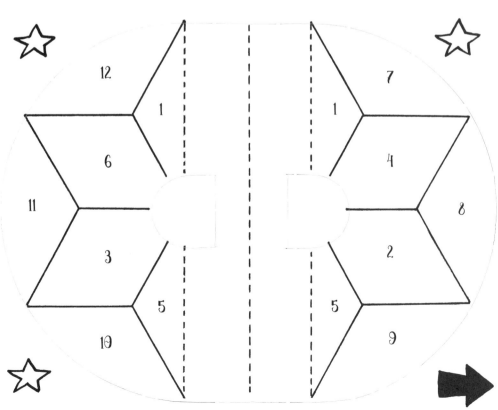

Things appear coloured because they reflect specific wavelengths of visible light into our eyes. Red objects reflect red light, green objects reflect green light, and so on.

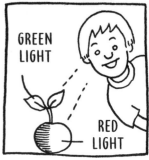

GREEN LIGHT

RED LIGHT

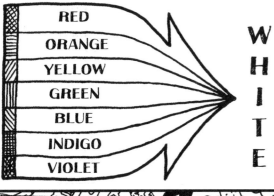

RED
ORANGE
YELLOW
GREEN
BLUE
INDIGO
VIOLET

WHITE

Objects that reflect all the colours of the rainbow appear white. Objects that absorb all the colours appear black.

HOW TO MAKE YOUR COLOUR WHEEL SPIN

'Mix' the colours on your colour wheel by spinning it rapidly. It should produce a white-ish hue.

1. Fold wheel and glue closed.

2. Tape two small coins of the same size underneath.

3. Tape a third coin or a glass marble in the centre slot.

4. Spin wheel on a smooth, hard surface.

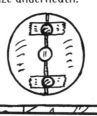

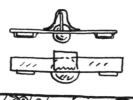

WOW!

ARTISTS HAVE BEEN USING COLOUR WHEELS FOR CENTURIES.

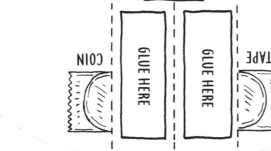

TAPE   GLUE HERE   GLUE HERE   COIN

NO GLUE

COIN   GLUE HERE   GLUE HERE   TAPE

Colours opposite each other on the colour wheel are called complementary.

RED ⟷ GREEN

BLUE ⟷ ORANGE

YELLOW ⟷ PURPLE

Placing these colours side by side makes them both appear more intense.

ROCK FACE

MAKE YOUR OWN AMAZING EASTER ISLAND ARTWORK.

Easter Island, or 'Rapa Nui', in the south-eastern Pacific Ocean, is famous for its giant stone statues.

MOAI

GLUE

The 'moai' sculptures were carved from volcanic rock over 500 years ago. Here's how to make a mini-moai.

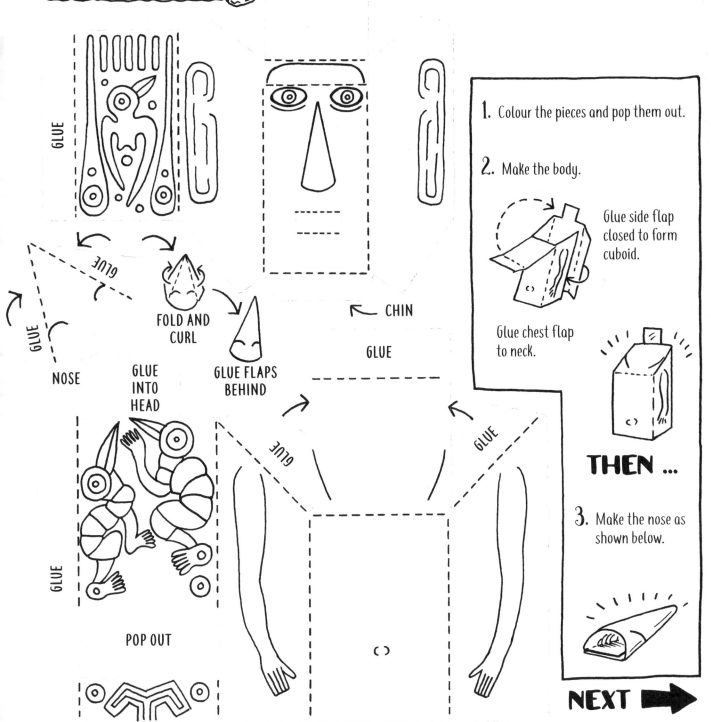

GLUE

FOLD AND CURL

NOSE

GLUE INTO HEAD

GLUE FLAPS BEHIND

CHIN

GLUE

POP OUT

1. Colour the pieces and pop them out.

2. Make the body.

   Glue side flap closed to form cuboid.

   Glue chest flap to neck.

THEN ...

3. Make the nose as shown below.

NEXT ➡

4. Construct the head.

Glue side-flap closed to form cuboid.

GLUE

Fold eyebrow ridge forwards, then glue back-of-head flap in place.

GLUE

5. Add nose.

Fold chin up.

6. Push lips out from inside, then glue head onto body.

FINISHED!

Most of the moai heads have massive bodies that lie hidden in the ground.

Give your moai legs by putting two fingers through the slot at the back.

HI!

EXPERTS THINK THE MOAI WERE CARVED BY THE RAPA NUI PEOPLE TO HONOUR THEIR ANCESTORS.

ENDLESS LANDSCAPE

The cards below show parts of an imaginary landscape. Colour them in, pop them out and place them side by side to make zillions of different scenes.

Colour the pictures however you like and carefully press out and make the models as shown over the page. Pop out and insert the special strip and you can make their eyes move for real.

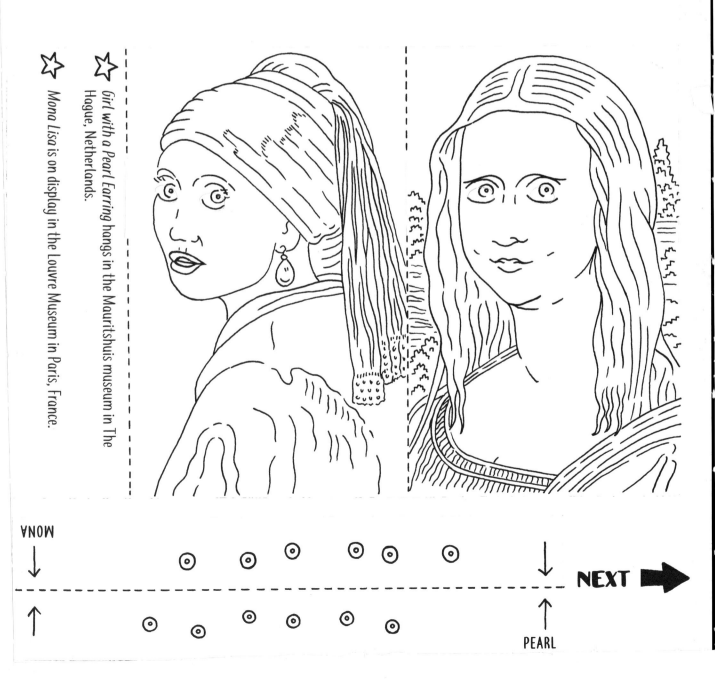

☆ ☆ *Girl with a Pearl Earring hangs in the Mauritshuis museum in The Hague, Netherlands.*

Mona Lisa is on display in the Louvre Museum in Paris, France.

MONA

PEARL

NEXT ▶

HOW TO MAKE YOUR MODEL

1. Fold the viewer.

   DON'T GLUE

2. Colour the eyes, then fold the strip in half.

3. Insert into slots the right way up.

4. Slide in and out.

5. You can also draw your own eyes on the reverse of the strip.

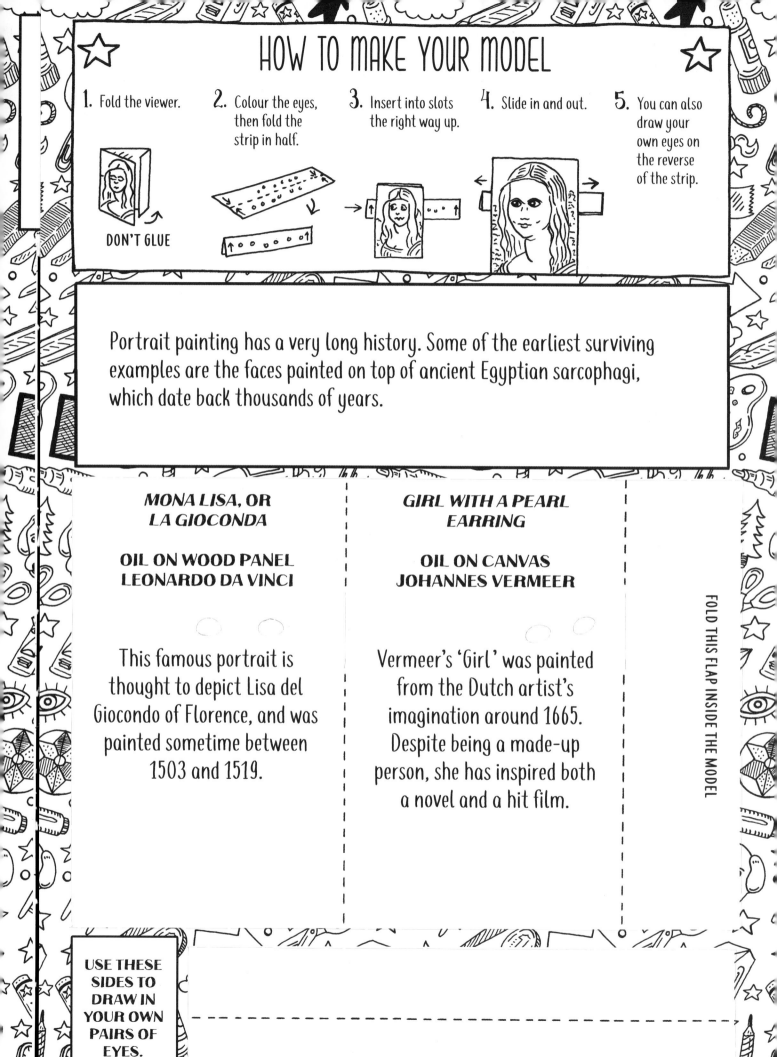

Portrait painting has a very long history. Some of the earliest surviving examples are the faces painted on top of ancient Egyptian sarcophagi, which date back thousands of years.

FOLD THIS FLAP INSIDE THE MODEL

MONA LISA, OR LA GIOCONDA

**OIL ON WOOD PANEL
LEONARDO DA VINCI**

This famous portrait is thought to depict Lisa del Giocondo of Florence, and was painted sometime between 1503 and 1519.

GIRL WITH A PEARL EARRING

**OIL ON CANVAS
JOHANNES VERMEER**

Vermeer's 'Girl' was painted from the Dutch artist's imagination around 1665. Despite being a made-up person, she has inspired both a novel and a hit film.

USE THESE SIDES TO DRAW IN YOUR OWN PAIRS OF EYES.

IN PERSPECTIVE

WHICH OF THESE THREE FIGURES LOOKS THE NEAREST?

IT'S AN ILLUSION!

Paintings are flat, yet the images on them can appear to have depth and three dimensions. This illusion is created using a technique called perspective. Objects that appear to be 'closer' to the viewer are drawn bigger, darker and in more detail than those further away.

VANISHING POINT

HORIZON

SEE FOR YOURSELF

1. Close one eye and hold up your thumbs in a line — one near, one far.

2. The closest thumb will seem bigger and more detailed.

Perspective became common in paintings from the 15th century onwards. Can you get it right? Colour the pieces below, then carefully cut them out.

PAINTING

CHAIRS

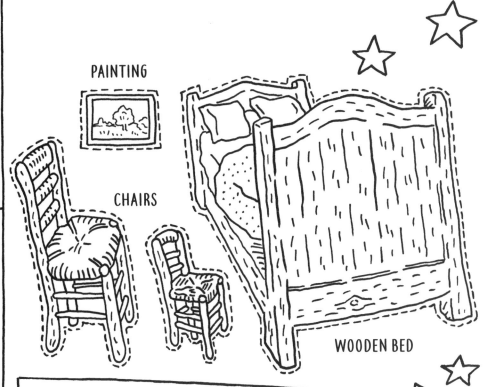

WOODEN BED

GRAB SOME GLUE, TURN THE PAGE.

Colour in the room, then glue the missing furniture on to this famous painting, *Bedroom in Arles*, using the rules of perspective.

Dutch artist Vincent van Gogh created this painting of his bedroom, in the French city of Arles, in the 1880s. Van Gogh's lines of perspective lead your eye to the open window at the back of the room.

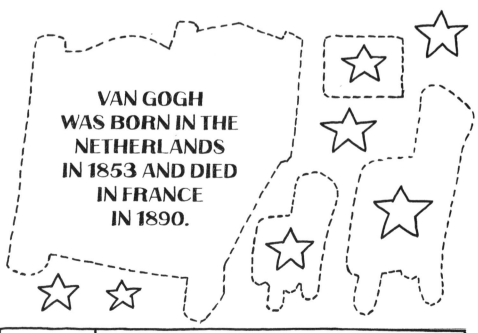

VAN GOGH
WAS BORN IN THE
NETHERLANDS
IN 1853 AND DIED
IN FRANCE
IN 1890.

**SELF-PORTRAIT
WITH
BANDAGED EAR**

Poor Vincent was often unwell and cut off his left ear and gave it as a gift.

FAB FACT! DESPITE BEING AN ARTISTIC GENIUS, VAN GOGH SOLD ONLY ONE PAINTING IN HIS LIFETIME.

OUT OF PERSPECTIVE

Italian Renaissance artists were the first to use 'one-point perspective' in their paintings. In this technique, all the lines in a picture lead to a single 'vanishing point' on a distant horizon.

CAN YOU ADD MORE TREES AND HOUSES?

ONE VANISHING POINT

OBJECTS OF EQUAL HEIGHT SHOULD GET SMALLER ALONG THE LINES OF PERSPECTIVE.

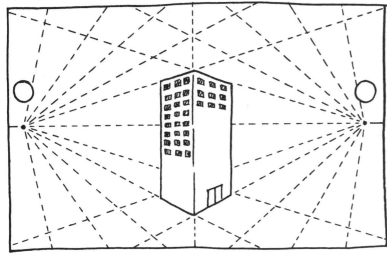

Pictures can have multiple points of perspective. Two-point perspective is brilliant for drawing skyscrapers. Why not add some more here?

HOGARTH AND HIS PUG, TRUMP, PAINTED IN 1745.

When art schools started teaching students the rules of perspective, lots of artists still made mistakes. To mock them, British painter William Hogarth (1697–1764) created an engraving called *Satire on False Perspective*, which was full of deliberate errors.

NEXT!

BE A PERSPECTIVE DETECTIVE

Circle all the perspective mistakes you can find in Hogarth's perspective-bending print. Then check your score against Trump's 'Paw-O-Matic' scoring system. A list of some of the errors is at the bottom of the page. Woof!

SCORE PAWS

0

1-9

10-19

20+

The church is crooked. The church is in the river. The bird is too big for the tree. The row of trees gets larger in the distance. The pipe and candle could not meet. The inn roof should not be visible. The church roof should not be visible. The inn sign hangs behind the trees. The inn windows are wrong. The man with the gun is shooting the bridge. The trees on the left cross strangely. The sheep and cattle get bigger away. The shed sides are wrong. The man is fishing too far away from the water. The left barrel is wrong. The big barrel is wrong. The floor tiles widen. The bridge gets nearer. There are lots of conflicting vanishing points. The river slopes.

WAVE FORM

COLOUR THE PICTURE.

The woodblock print *Under the Wave off Kanagawa* is probably Japan's most famous work of art. Also known as *The Great Wave off Kanagawa*, it was created by Katsushika Hokusai around 1831, and shows three boats carrying fish near the coastal town of Kanagawa. They are about to be engulfed by a monster wave with a million fingers.

HOKUSAI (1760—1849)

Origami is the Japanese art of paper folding. Cut out the sheet below and turn the page to learn how to fold your own Hokusai-style 'Great Wave' paper boat.

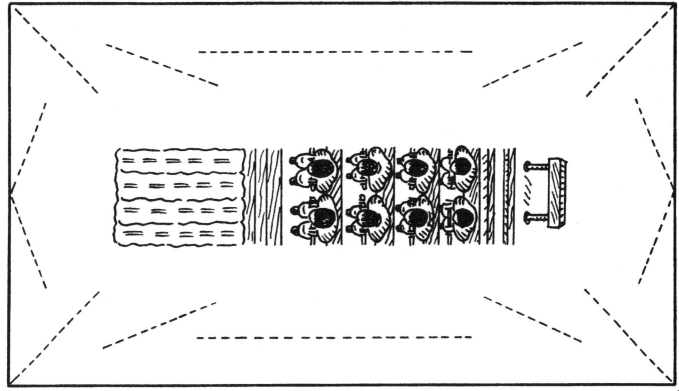

HOW TO FOLD YOUR HOKUSAI 'WAVE' BOAT

You can use these instructions to make more boats using any rectangle of paper.

1. Start with the title side up.

Fold long sides to the mid-line.

2. Fold all four corners to the mid-line.

Crease firmly.

3. Fold the ends to the mid-line once again.

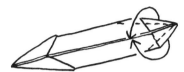

Crease firmly.

4. Fold the two sides to the mid-line.

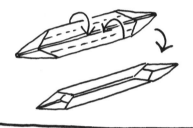

5. Open boat from the middle and turn inside out.

FINISHED BOAT!

Why not make a whole fleet of boats, float them in the bath and then send along your own 'Great Wave'?

FROM *UNDER THE WAVE OFF KANAGAWA*

BY KATSUSHIKA HOKUSAI, c. 1831

NAME GAME

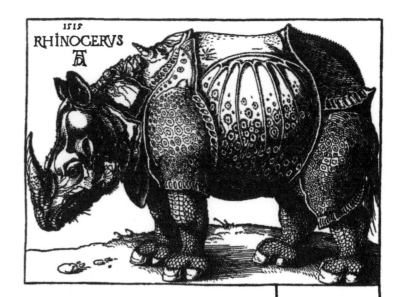

1515
RHINOCERVS

Artists have signed their works
for centuries. German engraver
Albrecht Dürer (1471–1528) combined his initials
to make a monogram. He used it to sign this engraving
of a rhino – an animal he never saw in real life.

Signing a work shows that it is finished. Signatures vary from full names to single
names or simple initials. The examples below are from artists featured in this
book. Can you work out who's who?

A. **DL**   B. **Meer**   C. *Vincent*   D. 北齋

E. P M   F. *Ed Munch*   G. *IOANNES HOLBEIN*

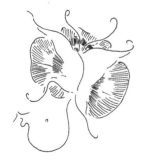

**AMERICAN ARTIST
JAMES ABBOTT MCNEILL
WHISTLER (1834–1903)
TURNED HIS INITIALS INTO
A MONOGRAM IN THE FORM
OF A BUTTERFLY WITH A
STINGING TAIL.**

A. Leonardo da Vinci B. Vermeer
C. Van Gogh D. Hokusai E. Piet Mondrian
F. Edvard Munch G. Holbein

**WHAT MIGHT YOUR
MONOGRAM LOOK LIKE?**

23

CRAFT YOUR OWN ARTIST
PABLO PICASSO

PICASSO, AGED 8

Many consider Pablo Picasso to be the greatest artistic genius of all time — an opinion Picasso himself would have echoed.

 Born in Andalusia, Spain in 1881, the young Picasso produced his first oil painting when he was just eight years old.

PICASSO IN 1912

Picasso was a prolific artist and created over 50,000 artworks in his lifetime — including prints, paintings, drawings, stage designs, ceramics and sculptures — all of which now fetch huge sums of money at auction.

Picasso had a very long career and changed his artistic style many times. He died in France in 1973 at the age of 91, but is still so famous that he has even had a model of car named after him.

NOW MAKE A PINT-SIZED PABLO!

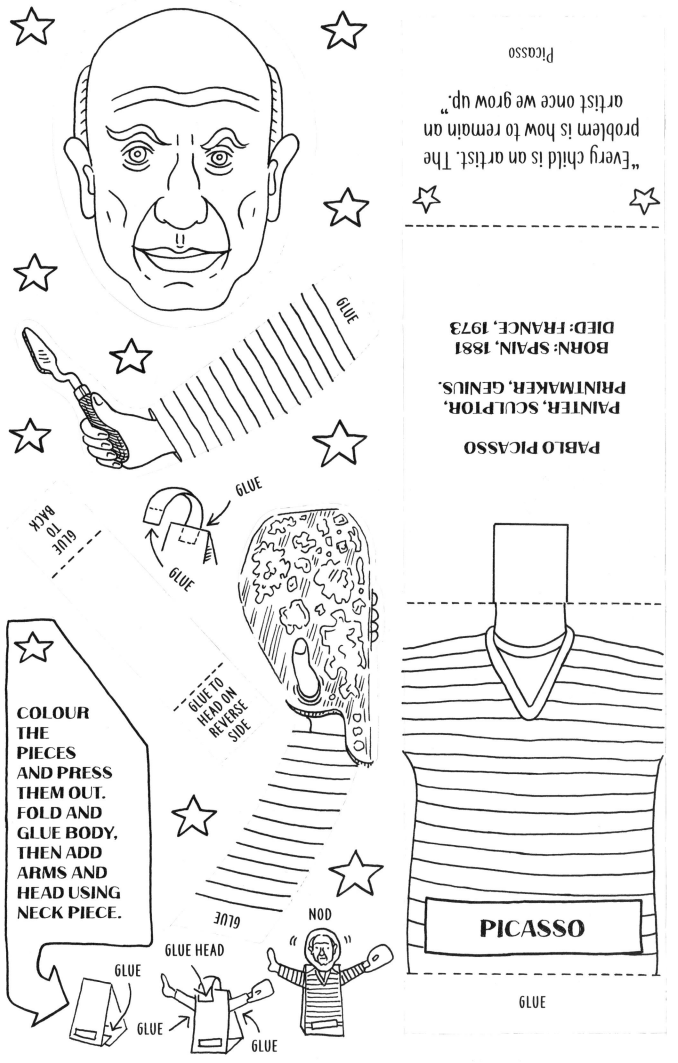

GLUE

GLUE

GLUE TO BACK

COLOUR THE PIECES AND PRESS THEM OUT. FOLD AND GLUE BODY, THEN ADD ARMS AND HEAD USING NECK PIECE.

GLUE TO HEAD ON REVERSE SIDE

GLUE

GLUE HEAD

GLUE

GLUE

GLUE

NOD

"Every child is an artist. The problem is how to remain an artist once we grow up."

Picasso

PABLO PICASSO

PAINTER, SCULPTOR, PRINTMAKER, GENIUS.

BORN: SPAIN, 1881
DIED: FRANCE, 1973

PICASSO

Picasso

GLUE

LEGEND HAS IT THAT
BABY PICASSO'S FIRST WORD
WAS 'LÁPIZ' – SPANISH
FOR 'PENCIL'.

THE ART WHIRL

MAKE YOUR OWN MINI SPIN PICTURES!

Spin pictures are a form of action painting. Paint is applied to a revolving surface and quickly spreads across it when it is spun. Pop out the pieces on this page to make your spinner.

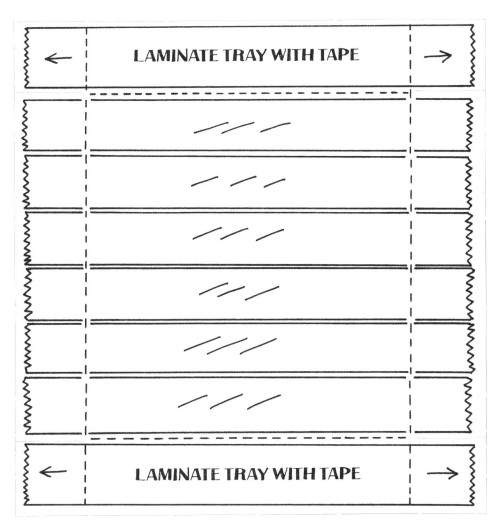

LAMINATE TRAY WITH TAPE

LAMINATE TRAY WITH TAPE

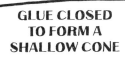

GLUE CLOSED TO FORM A SHALLOW CONE

GLUE

GLUE CONE TO UNDERSIDE OF TRAY

GLUE

GLUE ON TOP

1. Lay the tray piece flat and laminate with sticky tape to waterproof it.

OVERLAP THE STRIPS

2. Fold up into a tray and tape shut.

FOLD FLAPS AND TAPE

3. Finally, glue cone to underside.

DONE!

HOW TO USE YOUR MINI SPIN PAINTER

1. You will need some runny paints and the inserts on page 37.

2. Place paper insert in spinner.

3. Add blobs of paint on top.

4. Spin the painter, fast!

5. See the paint move.

6. Remove and dry your paintings.

⭐

REMEMBER

SPINNING PAINT CAN BE A BIT MESSY. WEAR AN APRON AND PUT DOWN OLD NEWSPAPER.

YOUR MINI SPIN PICTURES MIGHT LOOK LIKE THIS ...

ALFONS SCHILLING PIONEERED SPIN ART IN THE 1960S.

DAMIEN HIRST HAS ALSO EXPERIMENTED WITH SPIN PICTURES.

SEE PAGE 37

SPOKES PERSON

WHEEL RIM

BICYCLE WHEEL

MARCEL DUCHAMP

In 1913, French-American artist Marcel Duchamp (1887–1968) created *Bicycle Wheel* with an old bike wheel and a stool. It's a modern art icon, and thought to be the first ever moving sculpture.

POP OUT THE PIECES AND HOLES TO MAKE YOUR OWN MINI SPINNING MASTERPIECE.

STOOL SEAT

WHEEL RIM

2. Glue   Glue

MAIN SPOKES

GGGGGGGGGGGGGGGGGG

Glue under

MAIN SPOKES

GGGGGGGGGGGGGGGGGG

Glue under

1. Glue one side of the spokes under the other, to make two shallow cones.

GLUE ON HERE

GLUE SEAT HERE

KITCHEN STOOL

BICYCLE WHEEL FORKS

NEXT

3. Make the wheel.

Glue rims on to spoke tabs.

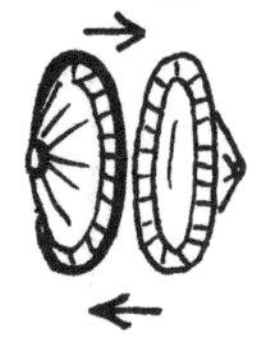

Glue the two wheel halves together.

4. Make the forks.

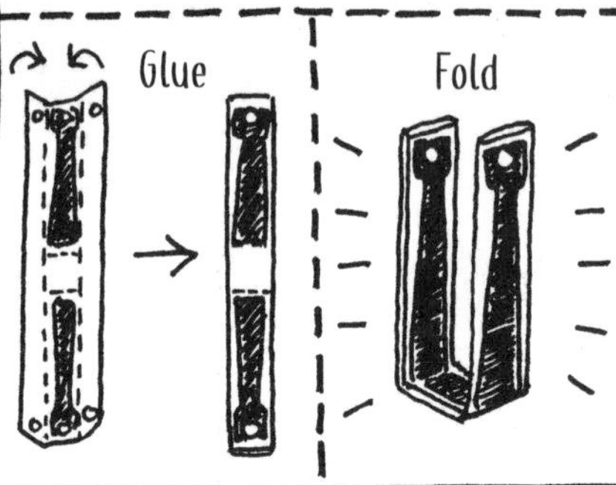

Glue   Fold

5. Assemble model.

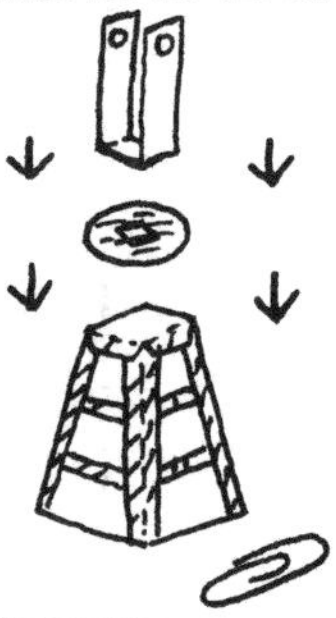

Glue forks on to seat.

Glue seat on to stool.

Next, grab a paperclip.

6. Add wheel using a paperclip axle.

SPIN!
☆
WOW!

Duchamp coined the term 'readymades' for art that was made using pre-existing objects.

DE STIJL TILES

PIET MONDRIAN (1872—1944)

Piet Mondrian was a key figure in the 20th-century Dutch art and design movement known as De Stijl ('The Style').

De Stijl was famous for its geometric designs. You can make your own using these tiles.

NEXT ...

31

1. Colour in some of the tiles using primary and secondary colours (see page 9), leaving about half of them plain white.

2. Place the tiles side by side to make millions of Mondrian-style designs.

Mondrian's artwork is famous for black-bordered rectangles and bright, vivid colours.

His style has often been borrowed and used to decorate

TRAINERS,

COSMETICS

AND DRESSES.

The De Stijl movement was founded in the Dutch city of Amsterdam in 1917 by several artists including Piet Mondrian, Vilmos Huszár (1884–1960) and Theo van Doesburg (1883–1931).

THEO VAN DOESBURG

'DE STIJL' MAGAZINE

The movement decreed that all art should be reduced to its purest forms, using only horizontal and vertical lines, with a palette limited to black, white and primary colours. It also published its own magazine.

Many of Theo van Doesburg's works had a maze-like appearance. Can you pick your way through the spaces in this Van Doesburg-style maze below? Colour it in afterwards.

IN ⇨

⇨ OUT

INSPIRED BY THEO VAN DOESBURG'S *COMPOSITION XIII* (1918)

MONA MANIA

Being the world's most famous painting can have its drawbacks. Lots of artists have made fun of Leonardo da Vinci's *Mona Lisa* (see page 15).

French cartoonist Eugène Bataille (1854–1891) gave her a long clay pipe in his 1887 version. Then, in 1919, pioneering surrealist artist Marcel Duchamp added a beard and moustache.

Duchamp (see page 29) doodled on a cheap postcard of the *Mona Lisa* to produce one of his most startling 'readymade' works of art. Now, you can do the same. Go crazy!

"HOW RUDE!"

LEONARDO DA VINCI

DALÍ

Another surrealist artist, Salvador Dalí (1904–1989), replaced the *Mona Lisa*'s face with his own. Try adding a photo or a drawing of yourself, and you too can be in the picture.

MEET A MASTER
BONE IDOL
MEXICAN PRINTMAKER

**JOSÉ POSADA
(AROUND 1900)**

José Guadalupe Posada (1851–1913) was an amazing Mexican printmaker and engraver whose work often featured bones, skeletons and skulls – known in Mexico as 'calaveras'.

ENGRAVINGS ARE DRAWINGS MADE BY CUTTING LINES INTO WOOD BLOCKS OR METAL SHEETS. THESE HOLD INK FOR PRINTING ON TO PAPER.

Posada used skeletons to portray people in the news in a funny or satirical way.

As well as humans, Posada also drew many bizarre bony beasts. What odd animal is this?

FIND OUT OVER THE PAGE!

DID YOU GUESS?

THIS IMAGE COMES FROM POSADA'S HUGELY POPULAR *CALAVERA OF THE ALLEY-CAT*.

DRAW YOUR OWN CALAVERA HERE!

Posada's signature can often be spotted hidden in his engravings.

POSADA

La Calavera Catrina (*The Elegant Skull*) is Posada's most famous work. It inspires the beautifully dressed skeletons in Mexico's annual 'Day of the Dead' festivities.

COLOUR THE HAT.

MAKE YOUR OWN 'DAY OF THE DEAD' MASK

JUST INSIDE THE FRONT COVER OF THIS BOOK IS A CATRINA-STYLE SKULL MASK TO MAKE AND WEAR! YOU CAN EMBELLISH YOUR MASK WITH YOUR OWN DESIGNS, GEMS, FEATHERS AND OTHER DECORATIONS.

SPIN PICTURE INSERTS

☆ Use these inserts in the spin painter on page 27. Copy their shape and you can also make your own.

☆ The folded sides help keep paint off the walls of your spin painter. Don't let it get wet and soggy.

☆ Dry your pictures flat. Once dry, you can cut off the sides and then add to your pictures in any way you like!

CAREFULLY CUT THEM OUT WITH SCISSORS.

MORE! ☆

FAB FACT 1

MODERN BRITISH ARTIST DAMIEN HIRST (BORN 1965) WAS INSPIRED TO MAKE SPIN PICTURES AFTER SEEING THEM MADE ON A CHILDREN'S TV SHOW.

FAB FACT 2

ARTISTS SOMETIMES MAKE SPIN PICTURES BY SPINNING A CANVAS ON TOP OF A FAST-MOVING POTTERY WHEEL.

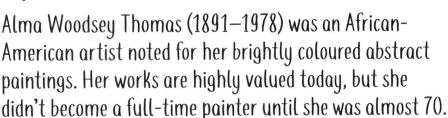

ABSTRACT ALMA

YOUNG ALMA

Alma Woodsey Thomas (1891–1978) was an African-American artist noted for her brightly coloured abstract paintings. Her works are highly valued today, but she didn't become a full-time painter until she was almost 70.

Alma worked as a school teacher for most of her adult life, painting in her spare time. At the age of 75, she studied the striking green leaves of a holly tree and this changed her style of painting. She soon began producing colourful, abstract works.

ALMA IN 1976

This mosaic-like pattern is inspired by Alma's series of paintings with concentric rings of colour.

COLOUR EACH RING A VIVID HUE TO PRODUCE YOUR OWN ALMA-STYLE ABSTRACT.

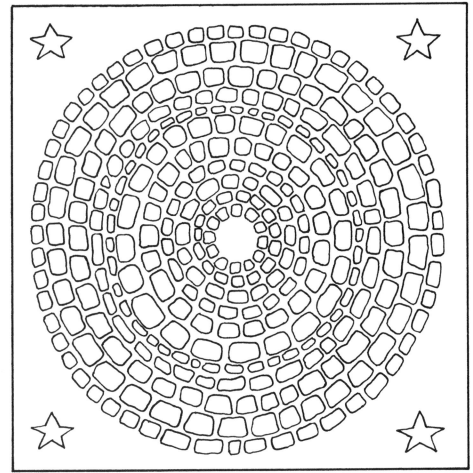

SCREAM TIME

☆

The Scream by Norwegian artist Edvard Munch (1863–1944) is a world-famous image. Munch created four versions of the picture between 1893 and 1910, in oils and in pastels.

COLOUR THE PICTURE.

☆

EDVARD MUNCH

☆

The Scream shows a strange howling figure on a cliff-edge walkway against a swirling orange sky, watched by two other mysterious figures lurking in the background. What do you think it could mean?

☆ One version of *The Scream* sold for 119.9 million US dollars in 2012. Today the picture even has its own emoticon, and has often been imitated, including in the poster for hit comedy film *Home Alone*.

NOW MAKE YOUR OWN 'SCREAM' PUPPET.

RIGHT ARM

Insert into right slot

LEFT ARM

Insert into left slot

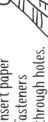

Insert flap under to close

Move arm ends up and down to make arms move

REMOVE STRIP

This model is based on a black and white print Edward Munch made of *The Scream* in 1895.

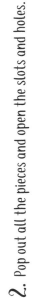

1. Colour the model, including both arm pieces.

2. Pop out all the pieces and open the slots and holes.

3. Fold card.

4. Insert arms into slots.

5. Insert paper fasteners through holes.

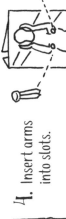

IT'S A SCREAM!

NEXT!

ARMS GO IN

ARMS GO OUT

6. Flatten fasteners inside.

7. Curl up arm ends.

8. Insert through back slot.

9. Fold flap closed.

10. Move arm ends up and down together at the back.

DONE!

PUP ART

American artist Andy Warhol (1928–1987) was a major figure in the 'pop art' movement of the 1950s and 1960s.

Pop art looked to TV, movies and everyday products for its inspiration.

Warhol made lots of brightly coloured prints of famous people, from actress Marilyn Monroe to Queen Elizabeth II.

Turn the page to see how to use these doggy stencils and make your own Warhol-inspired 'pup' art.

USE THESE STARS TO POSITION THE STENCILS

PRINT THIS PUP

1

2

3

ANDY WARHOL

Your print is of a dachshund dog.

Warhol loved dachshunds. He had two, called Archie and Amos.

WHAT IS YOUR PUP CALLED?

1. Pop out the stencils.

2. Place stencil number 1 on a piece of paper. Use a light-coloured paint or coloured pencils to fill in the spaces.

3. Use stencil 2 and then stencil 3 to repeat the process.

   Make sure the stars line up, and use darker colours on top of the light background.

4. The finished print should look like this:

   WOOF!

5. Use different colour combinations to make lots of 'pup' art prints.

ON THE PLINTH

**MONUMENT
RACHEL WHITEREAD, 2001**

Since 1999, Trafalgar Square in London has showcased some of the world's most exciting public art — both funny and thoughtful.

The 4-metre-high stone plinth has displayed works by leading modern artists, including Antony Gormley and Rachel Whiteread. Whiteread's upside-down resin model of the plinth itself is shown here.

Make the mini plinth below, and display your own exciting artworks on top.

1. Pop out the model and fold it on the dotted lines.

2. Glue flaps underneath.

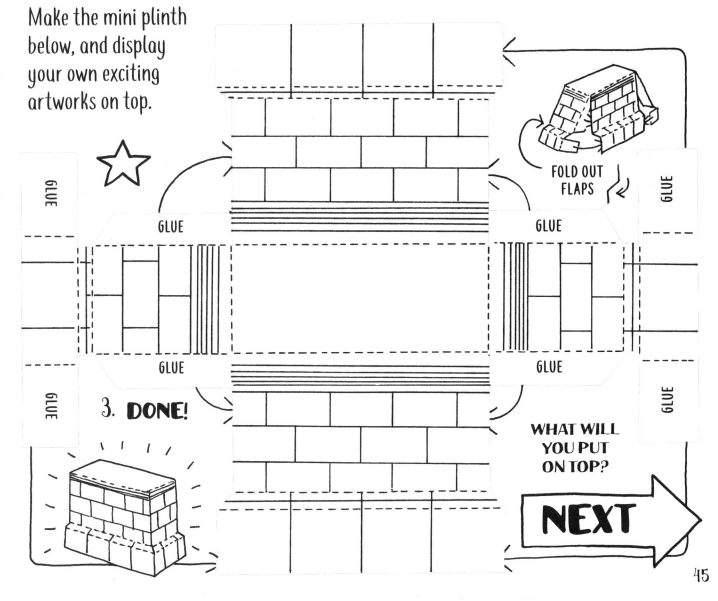

GLUE
GLUE
GLUE
GLUE
GLUE
GLUE
GLUE
GLUE

FOLD OUT FLAPS

3. **DONE!**

WHAT WILL YOU PUT ON TOP?

NEXT

SOME ARTISTS WHOSE WORK HAS BEEN ON THE PLINTH

RACHEL WHITEREAD (2001)

YINKA SHONIBARE (2010—2012)

KATHARINA FRITSCH (2013—2015)

HANS HAACKE (2015—2016)

DAVID SHRIGLEY (2016—2018)

Plinth artworks have included a giant model ship in a glass bottle,
the bronze skeleton of a horse, a child riding a rocking horse,
a massive blue cockerel and a huge thumbs-up.

WHAT WILL YOU DISPLAY ON YOUR PLINTH?

A PLASTIC BRICK MODEL?

A SOFT CLAY SCULPTURE?

A BIG YELLOW BANANA?

WHAT'S

ON

YOUR

PLINTH?

CRAFT YOUR OWN ARTIST
FRIDA KAHLO
ICONIC MEXICAN PAINTER

Frida Kahlo

"I paint because I need to."

FRIDA KAHLO
ARTIST, ICON.

BORN: MEXICO, 1907
DIED: MEXICO, 1954

FRIDA KAHLO

GLUE

GLUE

GLUE TO BACK

NECK PIECE (CURL)

GLUE TO HEAD ON REVERSE SIDE

47

Fold and glue the body into a triangle and pop up the parrot and the monkey. Then, add the arms and head.

GLUE

GLUE

GLUE

GLUE

FRIDA, AGED 12

Frida Kahlo is famous today as a great painter – particularly of some very intense self-portraits. Born in Mexico in 1907, her father, Guillermo, was a photographer and took many pictures of Frida and her sisters throughout their lives.

Sadly, Frida's life wasn't always happy. Aged eighteen, a terrible bus crash left her in constant pain. She began painting while recovering in her hospital bed.

FRIDA PAINTING IN BED AT HOME

Frida's self-portraits often featured her many animal companions. These included:

MEXICAN HAIRLESS DOGS   SPIDER MONKEYS   A FAWN   AN EAGLE

Frida died in 1954. Today she is more popular than ever. The interest in her life, art and image is known as 'Fridamania'.

I ♥ OP ART

BRIDGET RILEY

Op art — short for 'optical art' — is a style of art that uses contrasting patterns of lines, shapes and colours to create illusions in the eyes of viewers.

THIS IMAGE IS A TYPICAL OP ART DESIGN, INSPIRED BY BRIDGET'S WORK.

One of its most famous champions is Bridget Riley, a British op artist (born 1931). Her works have titles such as *Movement in Squares*, *Uneasy Centre* and *Composition with Circles*.

Fill in alternate circles in this Riley-style design using a strong black pen. Colour the others as you wish or leave them white. The final effect is mind-boggling.

TRY ROTATING THE PAGE!

THE EFFECT IS QUITE EXCITING.

WHAT'S YOUR ANGLE?

**THE AMBASSADORS
HANS HOLBEIN, 1533**

 The Ambassadors is a large oil painting by German artist Hans Holbein (c. 1497–1543). The image shows two rich diplomats with luxury items showing their wealth, along with a strange stretched object (arrowed) in the foreground. But what is it?

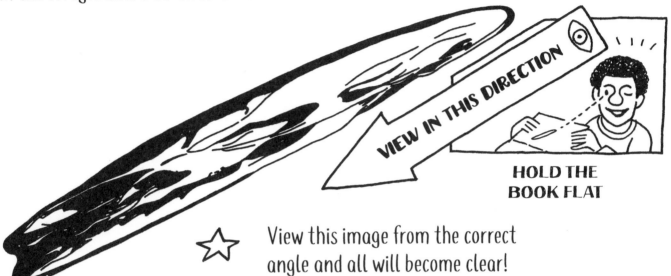

**HOLD THE
BOOK FLAT**

 View this image from the correct angle and all will become clear!

This distorted drawing is a famous example of 'anamorphic' art. Below is a simple grid method for making similar images. Check it out, then turn the page.

1. Draw an image on to a square grid. Then, guided by the squares, copy it on to a stretched version of the same grid.

2. Either rub out the grid lines or copy the image on to more paper. Now view it!

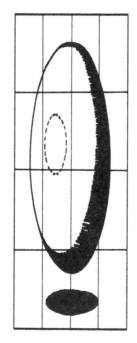

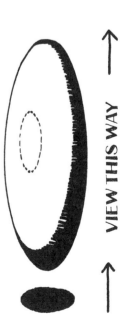

VIEW THIS WAY

Now have a go at creating your own anamorphic art. First, draw a design on to the square grid – not too elaborate – then copy each square on to its corresponding place on the stretched grid, allowing for the distortion. Finally, trace or redraw to get rid of the grid.

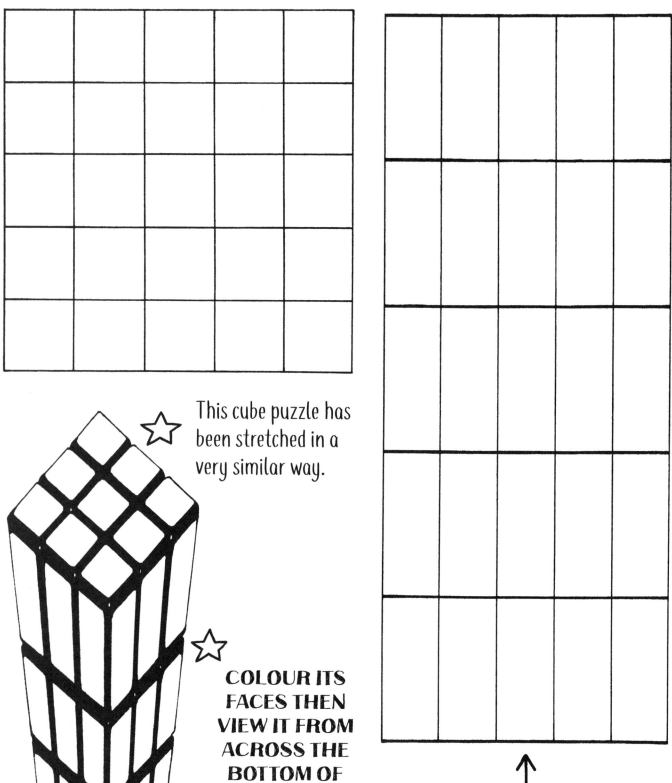

This cube puzzle has been stretched in a very similar way.

COLOUR ITS FACES THEN VIEW IT FROM ACROSS THE BOTTOM OF THE PAGE. WOW!

You can check your drawing as you go along by looking from this direction.

BRICK TRICK

ROA (born around 1976) is the tag used by a mystery street artist from Belgium. A tag is a type of signature used by graffiti artists. Who is he?

ROA is famous for his giant murals of animals all over the world — often showing their insides.

Sometimes, due to the shape of the walls, his murals reveal another image when viewed from a different direction.

This trick is known as 'lenticular art'. You can make your own ROA-style mural using the instructions over the page.

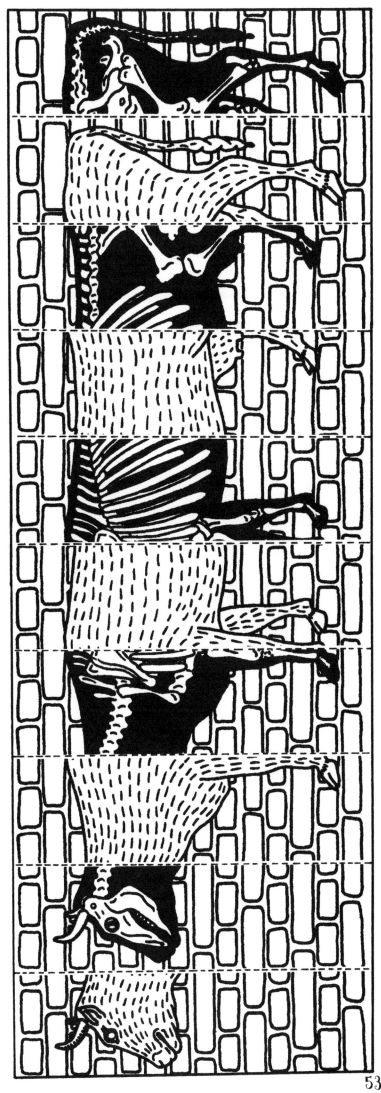

53

1. Colour and carefully cut out the strip.

2. Fold up and down on alternate crease lines.

VIEW FROM EACH SIDE

LEFT

RIGHT

SOME OTHER FAMOUS STREET ARTISTS

KEITH HARING
USA
(1958—1990)

'LADY PINK'
ECUADOR/USA
(BORN 1964)

'FALKO ONE'
SOUTH AFRICA
(BORN c. 1973)

'BANKSY'
UNITED KINGDOM
(IDENTITY
UNKNOWN)

NOW TRY DRAWING YOUR OWN LENTICULAR PICTURE.

YOU'VE BEEN FRAMED!

Make a simple paper frame that can magically transform an image into a work of art.

CHARLES RENNIE MACKINTOSH

1. Colour and carefully cut out the template along the solid lines.

2. Remove the central section with scissors or a craft knife.

CAREFUL!

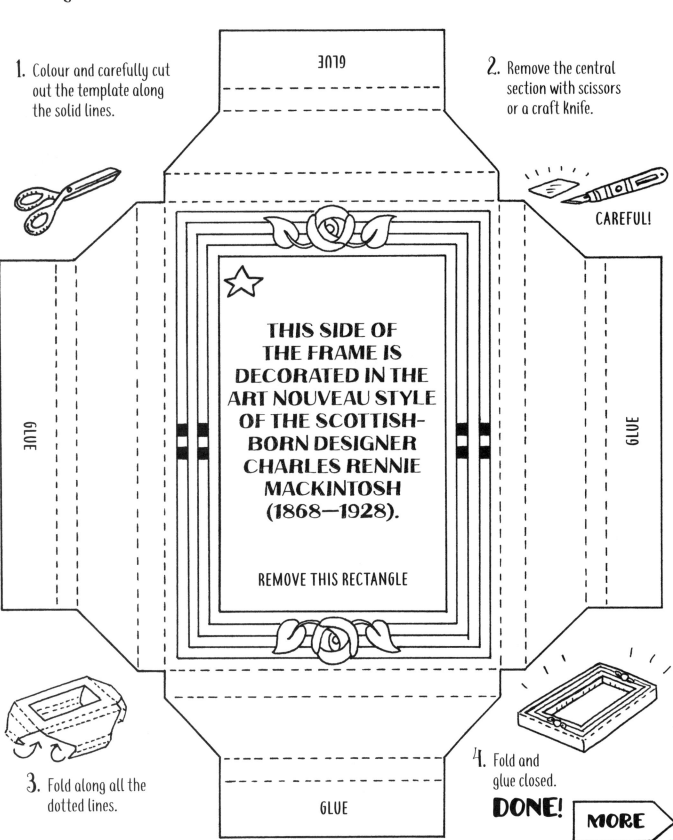

GLUE

GLUE

GLUE

THIS SIDE OF THE FRAME IS DECORATED IN THE ART NOUVEAU STYLE OF THE SCOTTISH-BORN DESIGNER CHARLES RENNIE MACKINTOSH (1868—1928).

REMOVE THIS RECTANGLE

3. Fold along all the dotted lines.

GLUE

4. Fold and glue closed.

DONE!

MORE

1. Try placing it over your own artworks, as well as pictures in books, magazines and papers.

2. Strangely, the simple act of framing an image can change how we see it. It can transform it into a work of art.

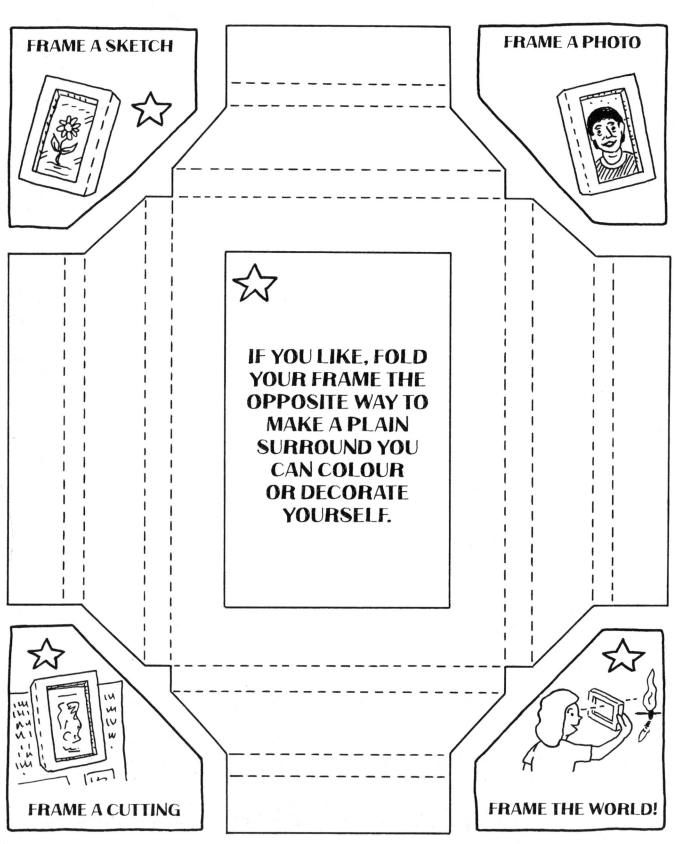

FRAME A SKETCH

FRAME A PHOTO

IF YOU LIKE, FOLD YOUR FRAME THE OPPOSITE WAY TO MAKE A PLAIN SURROUND YOU CAN COLOUR OR DECORATE YOURSELF.

FRAME A CUTTING

FRAME THE WORLD!